ELECTRIC BIKES

Jessica Rusick

Big Buddy Books
An Imprint of Abdo Publishing
abdobooks.com

abdobooks.com

Published by Abdo Publishing, a division of ABDO, PO Box 398166, Minneapolis, Minnesota 55439.

Printed in the United States of America, North Mankato, Minnesota
052023
092023

Design: Sarah DeYoung, Mighty Media, Inc.
Production: Mighty Media, Inc.
Editor: Katherine Chu
Cover Photograph: talevr/iStockphoto
Interior Photographs: ABB Photo/Shutterstock Images, p. 27; CL Shebley/Shutterstock Images, p. 23; GoConrad/Wikimedia Commons, p. 15; Gocycle, Karbon Kinetics Ltd., pp. 18–19, 28 (Gocycle G4); gunnsteinlye/Flickr, p. 11; Joseph Agustin Photo/Yamaha Bicycles, pp. 13, 29; koldo_studio/Shutterstock Images, p. 9; Mark Taylor Cunningham/Shutterstock Images, p. 21; RyanJLane/iStockphoto, p. 5; seanerino/Reddit, pp. 25, 28 (RadCity 5 Plus); SimonSkafar/iStockphoto, p. 7; TDowrick/Wikimedia Commons, p. 17
Design Elements: octopusaga/Shutterstock Images (hexagon pattern); Vlad Malinovskij/Shutterstock Images (lightning bolt icon); Zoa.Arts/Shutterstock Images (lightning)

Library of Congress Control Number: 2022948828

Publisher's Cataloging-in-Publication Data
Names: Rusick, Jessica, author.
Title: Electric bikes / by Jessica Rusick
Description: Minneapolis, Minnesota : Abdo Publishing, 2024 | Series: It's electric! | Includes online resources and index.
Identifiers: ISBN 9781098291518 (lib. bdg.) | ISBN 9781098277970 (ebook)
Subjects: LCSH: Electric bicycles--Juvenile literature. | E-bikes--Juvenile literature. | Electric vehicles--Juvenile literature. | Mopeds--Juvenile literature. | Transportation--Juvenile literature.
Classification: DDC 388--dc23

CONTENTS

CHAPTER 1

AN ELECTRIC BOOST

A cyclist pedals up a hill. The hill is steep, but her legs don't grow tired. That's because she is riding an electric **vehicle** (EV)! As the cyclist pedals, an electric **motor** gives her bike an extra boost of power. This helps the cyclist climb the hill with ease!

FAST FACT

Electric bicycles were invented in the late 1800s. But the rising popularity of gas cars that century made electric bikes less appealing. So, only a few were produced.

Electric bikes help people ride farther and faster than they can on regular bikes.

CHAPTER 2

WHY ELECTRIC?

Electric bikes (e-bikes) have grown in popularity since the 2000s for a few reasons. Gas **vehicles release** gases that harm Earth. And buying gas is **expensive**.

An e-bike's **motor** is powered by electricity. The electricity is stored in **rechargeable batteries**. Charging an e-bike costs less than buying gas. E-bikes do not release harmful gases.

An e-bike's batteries are charged by plugging the battery pack into a special charger.

CHAPTER 3

E-BIKE BASICS

Most modern e-bikes use **lithium-ion batteries**. They are light and charge quickly. Most e-bikes have a throttle and pedal **assist**. The throttle makes the e-bike move without pedaling. Pedal assist turns the **motor** on when a rider pedals. This makes it easier to pedal.

FAST FACT

In the US, it is illegal for e-bikes to go faster than 20 miles per hour (32 kmh) when using only the throttle.

People ride e-bikes for transportation and fun. During the COVID-19 pandemic, riding e-bikes was a popular and safe outdoor activity.

CHAPTER 4

YAMAHA

In 1993, Japanese company Yamaha made an e-bike with pedal **assist**. By 2016, the company had sold 2 million e-bikes in Japan.

In 2018, Yamaha began selling e-bikes in the US. Buyers liked that the e-bikes were strong and sturdy.

FAST FACT

E-bikes were popular in China and Japan before becoming popular in the US.

By 2008, Yamaha had sold 1 million e-bikes.

In 2022, Yamaha **released** a new e-bike in the US. The CrossCore RC had a newly **designed motor**. It was quieter but powerful.

The CrossCore RC's top speed was 28 miles per hour (45 kmh) with pedal **assist**. And it could fully charge in four hours. The CrossCore RC received positive **reviews** for its motor and comfortable ride.

The CrossCore RC cost $3,099 upon release. On low pedal assist mode, it could travel more than 100 miles (161 km) on one charge.

CHAPTER 5

GOCYCLE

New e-bike companies formed during the 2000s. British **engineer** Richard Thorpe founded Karbon Kinetics Limited (KKL) in 2002.

In 2009, KKL **released** the Gocycle G1. Buyers loved the e-bike's **design**. Unlike other e-bikes, the Gocycle's chain was inside its frame. This made the e-bike look sleek. It also meant that riders never had to clean or **repair** the chain!

Richard Thorpe left his dream design job at McLaren Cars to start KKL. His goal was to make the perfect e-bike.

KKL **released** more Gocycle models over time. The Gocycle G4 came out in 2022. It featured an improved **motor**. The motor made the G4 move faster than KKL's earlier models. This made pedaling up steep hills easier!

The G4 could also fold up for easy storing. Riders liked this new e-bike because it was powerful and easy to use.

Gocycle won the Best Electric Bike award at Eurobike in 2009 and 2012.

GOCYCLE G4

Starting price: $3,499

Top speed: 20 miles per hour (32 kmh)

Range: Up to 40 miles (64 km)

Charging time: 3 hours

Weight: 38.8 pounds (17.6 kg)

Statistics from 2023 model

Battery

Throttle
Dashboard (shows speed, battery level, and other information)
Gocycle
Motor
Charging port

CHAPTER 6

RAD POWER BIKES

American teenager Mike Radenbaugh founded Rad Power Bikes in 2007. Radenbaugh started by changing his customers' regular bikes into e-bikes.

In 2015, Rad Power Bikes **released** its first e-bike, the RadRover. **Reviewers** felt the e-bike was **affordable** and had a good **motor**. The e-bike also had thick tires. They made the ride smooth and comfortable.

It only took Radenbaugh 30 days to raise $320,000 to start building his first e-bike, the RadRover!

CHAPTER 7

RADCITY 5 PLUS

By 2019, Rad Power Bikes was the largest e-bike manufacturer in the US. In 2021, the company **released** the RadCity 5 Plus.

The RadCity 5 Plus had a range of 50 miles (80 km) on one charge. It could take up to seven hours to **recharge**. The e-bike also came with tires that helped make it more **efficient**.

In 2019, Rad Power Bikes released the RadRunner. Buyers could choose what features they wanted to add to the bike.

Reviewers liked the strong **motor** and comfortable ride of the RadCity 5 Plus. Buyers were also pleased with the e-bike's less **expensive** price of $1,999. And they liked the bike's quick brakes. Many buyers said it was the best e-bike for city riding.

The RadCity 5 Plus came with a redesigned motor and battery.

CHAPTER 8

THE FUTURE'S ELECTRIC

E-bikes have exploded in popularity. Since 2020, e-bikes have outsold electric cars in the US. This trend may continue in the **future**.

Meanwhile, **researchers** are improving e-bike **batteries**. New batteries will last longer and help e-bikes charge faster. In the future, e-bikes may rule the road!

Experts predict about 10 million e-bikes could be sold in Europe each year by 2025.

TIMELINE

1993
Yamaha makes an e-bike with pedal **assist**.

2002
Karbon Kinetics Limited (KKL) is founded.

2007
Rad Power Bikes is founded.

2009
KKL **releases** the Gocycle G1.

2015
Rad Power Bikes releases its first e-bike, the RadRover.

2021

Rad Power Bikes **releases** the RadCity 5 Plus.

2018

Yamaha begins selling e-bikes in the US.

2022

Yamaha releases the CrossCore RC. KKL releases the Gocycle G4.

GLOSSARY

affordable—having a cost that is not too high.

assist—an act or action that helps someone.

battery—a small container filled with chemicals that makes electrical power.

design (dih-ZINE)—to make a plan for how something will appear or work. Such a plan is called a design.

efficient—capable of producing desired results especially without waste (as of time or energy).

engineer (ehn-juh-NIHR)—a person who is trained to apply scientific knowledge to a practical purpose such as building machines or buildings.

expensive—having a high price.

future (FYOO-chuhr)—a time that has not yet occurred.

lithium-ion battery—a rechargeable battery that uses lithium ions as the primary component.

motor—a machine that produces motion or power for doing work.

recharge—to become charged again. Rechargeable means that something is able to be charged again.

release—to let go or make available to the public.

repair—to fix something.

researcher—a person who carefully studies a subject in order to learn facts about it.

review—a statement of thoughtful opinion. A reviewer is a writer of reviews.

vehicle—something used for carrying persons or large objects. Some examples of vehicles are cars, trucks, boats, and airplanes.

ONLINE RESOURCES

To learn more about electric bikes, visit abdobooklinks.com. These links are routinely monitored and updated to provide the most current information available.

INDEX